Vitamins!
What Foods Give You Which Vitamins
Healthy Eating for Kids
Children's Diet & Nutrition Books

PRODIGYWIZARD
BOOKS

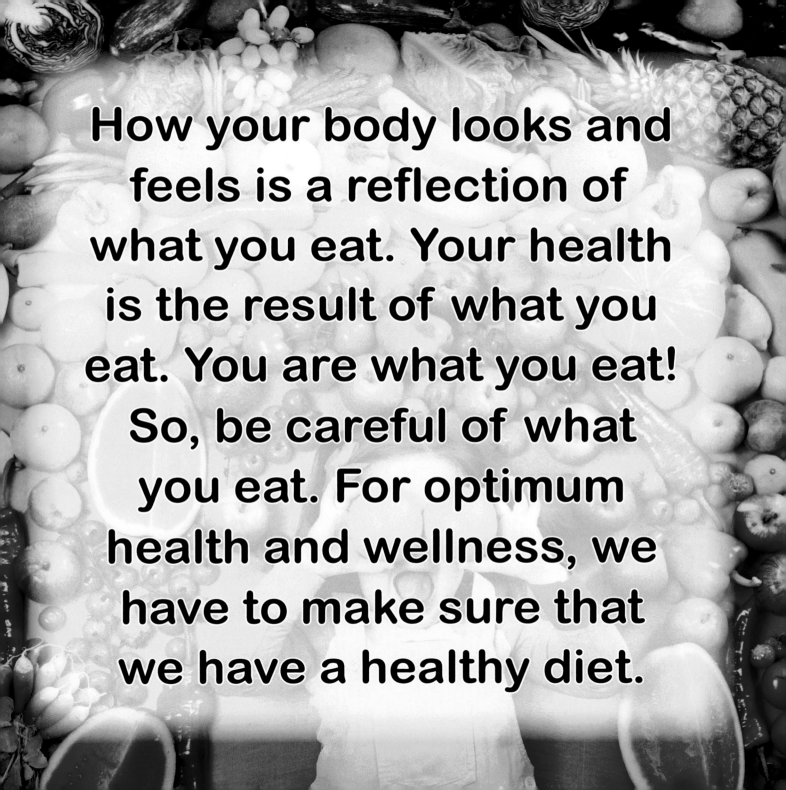

How your body looks and feels is a reflection of what you eat. Your health is the result of what you eat. You are what you eat! So, be careful of what you eat. For optimum health and wellness, we have to make sure that we have a healthy diet.

The foods we eat give our body the nutrients it needs so our organs and body parts can function well. The nutrients found in these foods aid us in our daily life.

Foods rich
in Vitamin A

Our body needs Vitamin A to maintain healthy teeth, bones, skin and soft tissues. This vitamin acts as a shield that keeps the body away from bacterial and viral infections. Vitamin A also prevents night blindness. It also keeps our hair and nails healthy.

The foods that are rich in Vitamin A are carrots, spinach, apricots, sweet potatoes, kale, collard greens and winter squash.

Foods rich
in Vitamin B

Vitamins B6, B12 and B9 (folic acid) are needed in our system to assist proper nerve function. They also help in the synthesis of DNA and in the formation of red blood cells. These vitamins help maintain brain functions.

The foods that are rich in Vitamin B are eggs, meat, poultry, fish, seafood like oysters and mussels, and milk. The foods rich in folic acid are leafy green vegetables, poultry, and oranges and grapefruits.

Foods rich in Vitamin C

Vitamin C is also known as ascorbic acid. It is a powerful antioxidant. It protects the health of cells and improves iron absorption. This vitamin is also needed in promoting teeth and gums and healing wounds.

Foods that are rich in Vitamin C include papaya, strawberries, citrus fruits, bell peppers, broccoli, dark leafy greens and Brussels sprouts.

Foods rich
in Vitamin D

This unique vitamin can be created by our body from the sunlight. Vitamin D is very important for bone health, calcium absorption and immune system health. This vitamin can also decrease the risk of colorectal cancer, according to the National Cancer Institute.

The foods high in Vitamin D are milk, eggs, shiitake mushrooms and some seafoods like herring, catfish, oysters, salmon and trout.

Foods rich in Vitamin E

This vitamin is a powerful antioxidant along with vitamin C. It protects body cells from damage. It helps the body to use vitamin K. It can also repair muscle cells.

Foods that are rich in Vitamin E are bell peppers, asparagus, spinach, turnip greens, Swiss chard, sunflower seeds and almonds.

Whatever we eat can impact our health. We should not just fill our stomach with the easiest food to get. Let's consider the nutrients that our chosen foods can give. The foods we take should give us numerous health benefits.

There is more to know about these vitamins and our health! Research and have fun!

Made in the USA
Middletown, DE
11 July 2023